ADAM MOUSE'S BOOK *of* POEMS

Adam Mouse Books by Lilian Moore

I'll Meet You at the Cucumbers
Don't Be Afraid, Amanda
Adam Mouse's Book of Poems

Lilian Moore

ADAM MOUSE'S BOOK *of* POEMS

drawings by Kathleen Garry McCord

A JEAN KARL BOOK

Atheneum   1992   New York

Maxwell Macmillan Canada
TORONTO

Maxwell Macmillan International
NEW YORK   OXFORD   SINGAPORE   SYDNEY

Atheneum
Macmillan Publishing Company
866 Third Avenue
New York, NY 10022

Maxwell Macmillan Canada, Inc.
1200 Eglinton Avenue East
Suite 200
Don Mills, Ontario M3C 3N1

Macmillan Publishing Company is part of the Maxwell Communication
Group of Companies.

First edition
Printed in the United States of America
10   9   8   7   6   5   4   3   2   1
The text of this book is set in 14 point Bembo.
The illustrations are rendered in pen and ink.
Book design by Tania Garcia

Library of Congress Cataloging-in-Publication Data
Moore, Lilian.
Adam Mouse's book of poems / Lilian Moore.—1st ed.
    p.   cm.
"A Jean Karl book."
Summary: A collection of poems about nature written by a mouse
named Adam.
ISBN 0-689-31765-4
1. Nature—Juvenile poetry.   2. Children's poetry, American.
[1. Nature—Poetry.   2. American poetry.]   I. Title.
PS3563.0622A44   1992
811'.54—dc20   91-42223

For Herman and his dad, Jonathan

CONTENTS

PART I

PART II

PART III

ADAM MOUSE'S BOOK *of* POEMS

PART I

Salamander,
as you wander
small and frail,
is it true that if you
lose it,
you grow another tail?

It's true.

In the caves and creeks and
ponds, where
you live and lay
your eggs,
is it true that if
you lose them
you grow new legs?

It's true.

And I find it very
helpful
that I do.

I'm green and
gold
in this bright sun.

This warm wet stone
is just my size.

I uncoil my
tongue   surprise
some flies.

Green and gold
and still as stone
I sit

listening.

Grass whispers a
warning and I
leap

into the glistening
muck of the
pond.

Sunned
Sated
Safe

Why should I want to be kissed?
Why should I want to be a prince?

Skunk
doesn't slink
but walks the earth
with a sense of worth

and wears with
pride
the bright white
stripe
on his inky
fur.

Skunk won't shrink
to face a
foe.
Gives fair warning
"Better go!"
and many a foe
has slunk
away.

Skunk is
spunky,
mild as well,
and what a tale his
tail
could tell!

Fireflies
Flash
Their cold gold glow
Upon the
Night,

Flickering,
Seeking.

Speaking
The language of
Light,
They find one
Another.

I know
I'm not soft
or furry

No one is in a
hurry
to hug me.

I know
I'm slow, a bit
stiff in the joints

but I don't
worry.

I'm a mellow
peaceful fellow

I have my good points.

Where
where
where
did I bury
that nut,

that sweet plump
nut that I carried
away?

Where
did I stop?
Where did I drop

that fat ripe nut
that I saved for
today?

Did I hide it
deep and far, or
near?

And why's a new green
nut tree growing
here?

Arabella the Cat
wears a collar
of bells, a
     ring-a-ling
     ding-a-ling
collar that tells
where Arabella
goes.

Arabella moves
softly
     in field and
     in furrow
softly,
so softly,
on pounce-ready toes.

Where's Arabella?

jing-a-ling
ting-a-ling

In nest and
in burrow

everyone knows!

HAWK

When hawk
rides
the sky

swoops
loops
swerves
into a cloud

glides
into a long
curve,

small creatures below
are
still,

holding
their
breath.

Will he soar
or
dive?

The baby wren
stands
in the nest.

Time to go.

But the world seems only
sky above and
earth below.

Clinging to the nest's
soft side,
feeling small,
until he dares
he cannot know

that he has wings and
will not fall.

Turtle Time

My time is
slow time,
old time,

the unhurried
time of
turtles
long ago.

Slowly,
I make my way.

Why hurry?

There was turtle time
before there was
people time.

FIDDLER

Cricket's wings
will never
lift him

from field
to soaring
flight.

Instead
they are his bow
and fiddle

making cricket
music
far into the

middle
of the soft summer
night.

PART II

The garden's green
with
teeny zucchini,
growing fatter
by the hour.

Teeny zucchini
growing fatter,
fat zucchini
growing
long.

Long
zucchini, growing
longer,
teeny zucchini,
growing strong.

Up to his
knees in
green zucchini
Help! cries the gardener.
Have a zucchini!

Please!

THE OLD WALL

See how these stones
trust
one another.
Stone resting on
stone
fitting curve and
edge
together.
Nothing but
stone
on
stone
shaping a wall
against
wind and weather.

I'm Dandelion

I scatter gold
on lawns.

I sprinkle meadows
with rays of
tiny suns.

I make puffs of
fog that sail the
wind

to everywhere, to
brighten
grass and shrub and reed.

And they call me a
weed!

The farmer tucks his tiny
seeds
into the earth and
waits—and
weeds.

Takes his hoe and
weeds.

Longs for
rain
and hopes for
sun,
longs for
sun
and hopes for
rain
and
waits and weeds.

Then one day there's
something green,
the promise of a pea or bean,
that seems to say
"Whew! We've come miles!"

Then at last the farmer smiles.

The small apple tree
hums
with bee buzz
with the beat of bee wings

It's Spring.

The small tree
hums and
sings

of apples in the Fall.

I come from the heart of
a flower.
Among many, I was one.
I have a secret power, and
I bring you the taste of the sun.

It's garden gossip
all day
long

cricket chatter
bee buzz babble

loud
bird song.

I look fierce
but ah, they
know.

I stand
tall
but they all
know.

I'm only
straw.
Can't scare a
crow.

A Pond Story

One day,
        said Old Frog,
deep in the mud
of the pond,
a seed took root.

What then?
said Little Frog.

Deep in the muck
of the pond
roots spread.

What then?

Out of the roots
long stems
swam up,
found the light,

and unfurled leaves
on the ripples of
the pond.

And then?

Ah, then,
with a queenly nod
to all,
the white flower of
the water lily
opened.

❦

The fog
comes down
from the hills

and there
are
no hills.

The fog
lies down
on the meadow

and there is
no
meadow.

The fog
wraps
the barn

and there is
no
barn.

We know
they are
there

the hills
the meadow
the barn—

Still
we peer
into the fog

just to be sure
just to be sure.

Under the fields
of grass
are
the tunnels,

the runways
where earthworms
wriggle their
long cool bodies

where sharp-clawed
moles
dig
blindly

where grasshoppers and
beetles
hide their secret
eggs,

the dark winding
tunnels of
a world
under a world.

From the far
hills
to the faraway
sea
I go.

I flow around
rocks
slip over
stones
and talk to
raindrops.

I carry splinters
of sunlight
and the shadows of
clouds.

Minnows and
sunfish
ride with
me.

Frogs
sit greenly
beside me.

I chatter with
deer
but I can't stay.
I'm on my way—
on my way
to the
sea.

Row on row,
you never hear the garden
grow.

Seeds split.
Roots shove and reach.
Earth heaves.

Leaves unfurl.
Stems pierce the
ground.

Pea pods fatten.
Vines
stretch and curl.

Such growing
going on
without a sound!

PART III

Hooray for light!
For this longest day and
shortest night.

Be up
today
with the rising
sun!

Fill like a
cup
with Summer light.

Watch the sky's first
pearly glow
chase away the sun-struck
moon.

Play in the sun-drenched
afternoon.
Play in an evening
bright as day.

Hooray for light!

I've watched a
cloud
nibble
a slice of moon.

I've seen the sky
at dusk
fill
with spilling sun.

And once
I saw a star,
just one
alone in all that sky.

The cloud
in the sky is
the cloud
in the river.

The sky's
blueness
lies there
too.

Tonight
the river will
receive a white
moon.

The sky is the
giver of
light
to the river.

Nothing quite
dry.
Sidewalks still gleam,

little rivers
stream
in the streets,

puddles hold pieces
of the morning
sky.

Now the rising sun
is glowing
on a small surprise

where

nudging the wet earth
in a cracked
sidewalk

mushrooms are growing.

Above the neon
glare, where words
flash and dance,

above the glowing
windows of tall
buildings,

above the runway
lights that call to
planes

rushing like
comets through
the
night sky,

a pale moon rises
and hopes to be
noticed.

The quiet here is
full of voices.

All those words on
all those shelves!

"Come closer," they whisper.
"Listen."

"We have much
to tell you—

stories of long ago,
tales of tomorrow.

What do you need
to know?

Ask us.
We love questions!"

❦

Waiting
is a road that
winds,

winds to a faraway
end.

No matter how you
hurry
the road has another bend.

INDEX

Lilian Moore's earlier books about Adam Mouse are *I'll Meet You at the Cucumbers* (about Adam's trip to the city to meet his pen friend Amanda) and *Don't Be Afraid, Amanda* (about Amanda's trip to the country). Lilian Moore herself lives in the country, but in the past she has lived in the city, so she can understand how both Adam and Amanda feel about the place they live, the adventures they share, and the friends—and dangers—they know

What reviewers have said about *I'll Meet You at the Cucumbers*:

"Offers children a glimpse of what love and friendship are all about."

—*Booklist*

"This [book] has masterful writing that manages to achieve a charming simplicity while making profound statements about the human condition. It will also be enjoyed as a lively animal fantasy."

—Starred, *School Library Journal*

"Adam's poems are small gems. . . .A fine read-aloud, and a perfect way to introduce poetry."

—*Kirkus Reviews*